T0193133

Mind-Heart
Connection

A Thought That Provokes the
Subconscious Mind into Actioning
a Program in the Conscious Mind
for a More Balanced Life.

David P. Ellis

BALBOA.
PRESS
A DIVISION OF HAY HOUSE

Copyright © 2018 David P. Ellis.
Designed by: David Ellis
Cover Graphics: Ciprian-Adrian Cerbu

All rights reserved. No part of this book may be used or reproduced by any means, graphic, electronic, or mechanical, including photocopying, recording, taping or by any information storage retrieval system without the written permission of the author except in the case of brief quotations embodied in critical articles and reviews.

Balboa Press books may be ordered through booksellers or by contacting:

Balboa Press
A Division of Hay House
1663 Liberty Drive
Bloomington, IN 47403
www.balboapress.com
1 (877) 407-4847

Because of the dynamic nature of the Internet, any web addresses or links contained in this book may have changed since publication and may no longer be valid. The views expressed in this work are solely those of the author and do not necessarily reflect the views of the publisher, and the publisher hereby disclaims any responsibility for them.

The author of this book does not dispense medical advice or prescribe the use of any technique as a form of treatment for physical, emotional, or medical problems without the advice of a physician, either directly or indirectly. The intent of the author is only to offer information of a general nature to help you in your quest for emotional and spiritual well-being. In the event you use any of the information in this book for yourself, which is your constitutional right, the author and the publisher assume no responsibility for your actions.

Print information available on the last page.

ISBN: 978-1-9822-0826-4 (sc)
ISBN: 978-1-9822-0830-1 (hc)
ISBN: 978-1-9822-0827-1 (e)

Library of Congress Control Number: 2018908147

Balboa Press rev. date: 07/24/2018

"If I have no honour
or integrity, then I
have nothing."

David Ellis

Contents

Dedication

Edward Joseph Ellis (Teddy). Over 100 years ago in 1916, a great man arrived on the planet, his name was, Edward. His friends and his wife, my Mum called him Teddy. To this day I have no idea why. Nonetheless, I loved the name as much as I loved the man.

He was the most honest, honourable, loving, non-judgemental and courageous man I have ever known. Edward was my Dad, and I miss him every day since he left our great planet to return home in 1997.

I live my life every day in the hope that one day I will possess the great qualities he once possessed and I can love as he loved, unconditionally.

As I reflect on my young life, I recall his embrace, his hugs, his great smile and the birthmark on his nose. I recall his tenderness as he would walk me to the bathroom as I stood on his feet so I would not get cold touching the floor.

Or the many nights I crawled in beside him when I could not sleep, he would greet me with loving open arms, cuddling me as I fell asleep in his embrace.

I remember his affection, great love and I recall his teaching, his wisdom, his caring and sometimes, even now, I can still sense his presence.

How time flies and how we don't realise what we have until it is gone.

I dedicate this book to my Dad, Teddy.

I Miss You.

About the Author

I live my life from the core belief of honour and integrity. Where I live, love and meet others, I expect that core belief to be respected and honoured.

Who am I?

I was born to Eileen and Edward Ellis who taught me that nothing mattered in life as long as you had love in your heart and lived with honour and integrity.

I am a simple man, with simple principles, I am not the sum of my achievements. I am not my past, and I am not my mistakes, I am not what I do or what I know. I am not what I own. I am simply, David.

A positive, heartfelt belief was inherent within me from a very young age that, *"I can do it"* and *"I can be what I want to be."* That belief drove me along my journey, and in that pursuit of *"I can,"* I was successful most of the time. However, sometimes I failed, and when I failed, I learned, before trying again. Each time I tried and believed in my heart that I would be successful, I was successful. But every time I used my head and thought the process through, or became fearful, I failed. The interesting thing here is, the more you fail, the more you fear failure and the more you fail. It's a problematic loop to escape.

During my earlier journey, I made mistakes - so many mistakes. I was incongruent with myself and did not live my truth. I lived a lie, and I was ashamed of who I was, and as a result, I hurt myself. More importantly, I hurt the people I loved. They were hurt, and it was my fault.

As I journeyed deeper into self with new learnings of universal energy and quantum physics, I became congruent with self and truthful to who I am. I vowed never to lie or hurt others again in the pursuit of my own identity, life goals or dreams.

The pain I felt after my Dad died left a void which I slowly filled with study. Studies into energy, holistic healing and the life hereafter. My first interest was a study in Colour Therapy, which opened the door for my new learning. I continued with more education embracing Crystal Therapy, REIKI, Hypnotherapy, Addiction Counselling, C.B.T, Stress Management, N.L.P, and a host more, I continue to learn today.

I practised as a therapist for 20 years and taught courses in Stress Management, The Power of the Subconscious Mind, Colour Therapy and Crystal Therapy at the Atlantis Institute in Ireland.

Over the past ten years, I have written many inspirational quotes, memes, blogs, and articles, which I have shared on my websites - www.ThePositiveMind.ie, www.AtlantisCentre.ie and www.DavidEllis.ie along with my social media platforms. I decided that I would combine my work and publish them in hard copy, to share the knowledge that has been imparted to me through my life experience, teaching career and as a therapist, hypnotherapist, and counsellor.

The inspiration to write my memes and quotes came from events in my day to day life. People I have met and places I have visited, these would resonate very strongly in my heart. As waves of learning would present themselves in the matrix of universal consciousness, I learned that these teachings were sporadic and not a regular occurrence. So I began to write my quotes, articles, and blogs as they occurred to me and I continue to do that today.

Introduction

There is a universal truth that our subconscious mind records everything we see, do and hear. It also manages our conscious mind including all our bodily functions and organs.

We impress into our subconscious mind a set of programs, positive and negative, that are activated by our conscious self-talk, thinking, desires, wishes, hopes, and emotions, unaware that the subconscious mind does not identify between positive or negative.

The subconscious mind then takes the information and creates a program based on the feedback and runs that program automatically without any further reference or consultation with the conscious mind.

This is why hypnosis is such a powerful tool in helping us in areas of weight loss, motivation, self-belief, self-esteem, self-image, addiction, self-healing, the list goes on and on.

The pioneering work of Dr Bruce Lipton established that cellular memory is also involved in the recording of our self-talk, thinking, desires, wishes, hopes, and emotions. [Fig I].

Cellular memory, as the name suggests, are memories that are stored in our cells, which in essence means that every memory is stored in every cell of our body. As each cell contains all memories, the same as a hologram, each piece includes the whole story.

When we affirm to ourselves, through low self-esteem, self-talk or negative thinking that we are stupid, wrong, fat or ugly, our subconscious mind will take that belief and run a program to create that manifestation.

On the other hand, if we affirm those positive affirmations, we begin to reprogram the subconscious to run a new program. Therefore, those affirmations that are positive, such as "I am happy" "I am thin" or "I am intelligent" will manifest if our affirmation is emotionally congruent with our heartfelt beliefs, desires, and wishes, and that the external environment is also in congruence with those desires.

What do we mean by "the external environment?" Allow me to explain, When the external environment is not corresponding with our desires, it becomes impossible for that desire to manifest. An example of an incongruent environment would be a desire to build a house in the heart of the desert with a lush green garden and a babbling brook.

We cannot manifest against what is natural in nature, and I express natural because we may believe illness is natural. However, when we consider that 97% of humans are born in full health, we see that being well is, in fact, the natural state of being and therefore when we get sick, we can change our state of being through our thought/feeling process.

As humans, we accept, as a heartfelt belief, what we are told by people whom we perceive as being experts. The doctor, for example, we consider to be an expert, and he is. So when the doctor tells us we are very sick, we accept what the doctor tells us.

Why? Because we feel sick and therefore we are vulnerable, and when we are vulnerable, we operate from our heart space.

Therefore, as a result of what the Doctor has told us, in our vulnerable state, a program immediately runs in our subconscious mind to facilitate our new heartfelt belief. This program runs automatically whether we are sick, or not sick. And once the program is running, we are then ill. In other words, once we accept what the doctor has told us, from our heart, we then affirm what has been said, our greatest fear manifests and the program runs.

We have no power over what runs and does not run, other than the conscious belief and heartfelt feeling that goes along with that belief.

What if we didn't believe/feel everything we were told? What if we became more mindful. In a state of mindfulness, there is a universal knowing of truth, and therefore we would already know what was truth and not fall prey to the belief of sickness.

By being mindful, we allow a natural connection to occur between the heart and the mind. The heart always knows the truth because the heart is void of the ego.

Through mindfulness, we become more in tune with ourselves and our source of energy. We become more discerning about what we are told and what is true and untrue.

This in no way suggests that the Doctor is not truthful, he is. But it's his truth. It's also important to realise that sometimes the Doctors truth and our own is indeed the same, but through mindfulness, we already would know this.

By being mindful, and if our truth is different to that of the Doctor, we could run a different program, a program based on wellness and health, a program based on living.

What might happen then? Might we get better instead of sicker?

Stress

Implications of Stress

When there is a disturbance in our energy field, when the heart is incongruent with the mind, this disturbance causes an energy imbalance. In turn, it causes distress in the body, this distress is stress as we know it.

What is Stress?

Stress is the number one cause of all human illness. Stress can mean different things to different people. Stress is often defined as a conflict between the demands placed on us and our ability to cope with those demands. The way we cope with those demands will depend on the way we think, our personality and our previous life experiences.

We live in a world where we hear about stress all the time. We know of the health issues it can cause, the depression, heart disease and the suicides that have occurred from stress, yet we seldom heed what we hear.

Stress is not a fad or a diminishing of one's coping abilities or strategies. It is a danger to us and needs to be dealt with when it is presented.

Triggers that cause Stress

Many things can trigger stress, including change. Changes can be positive or negative, as well as real or perceived. These changes may be recurring, short-term or long-term. Stress is the "wear and tear" we experience as we adjust to our continually changing environment, which creates the positive and negative physical and emotional effects.

Stress Accelerates Aging

Stress doesn't just make us feel older. It can speed up ageing. A study published in the Proceedings of the National Academy of Sciences found that stress can add years to the age of individual immune system cells. [Fig. II]. The study focused on telomeres, caps on the end of chromosomes. Whenever a cell divides, the telomeres in that cell get a little shorter and a little more time runs off the clock. When the telomere becomes too short, time runs out, The cell can no longer divide or replenish itself. This is a crucial process of ageing, and it's one of the reasons why humans can't live forever.

Good and Bad Stress

As with everything in the world, there is good and bad. Therefore there is positive and negative stress. A positive stress influence can help propel us into action. It can result in a new awareness and an exciting new outlook on a situation, event or life itself. Harmful stress, however, can have life-changing effects on our physical and mental health. Stress is compounded by nature and therefore builds upon itself. Without a coping mechanism, for every five minutes of stress encountered by the mind and body, we need to spend twelve hours in relaxation to bring the mind and body back into balance.

How we cope with Stress

People differ dramatically in the type of events we interpret as stressful and the way in which we respond to such stress. For example, driving a car can be extremely stressful for some people but for others, it's simply relaxing.

The ability to tolerate stress is linked to our individual personality, our relationships, energy levels, and emotional maturity. For instance, if we are introverted, we are generally more comfortable with fewer stimuli than if we are more extroverted. If we are in unhappy relationships, it is energy consuming, and therefore our energy levels become depleted and drained, the result is our resistance to stress is compromised. Also, when we are recovering from illness or simply tired at the end of the day, our ways of dealing with the world around us is less robust.

Freeze-Fight-Flight

The human "Freeze, Fight, Flight" response is written into our DNA. It's part of our blueprint, it's a primitive design to allow the body to quickly adapt to its environment, to survive.

During a freeze-fight-flight episode, breathing rate speeds up, nostrils and air passages in the lungs open wider to get more air in quickly. The heartbeat speeds up, blood pressure rises, sweating increases to help cool the body and blood and nutrients are concentrated into the muscles to provide extra strength.

Stress Hormones

Stress hormones, epinephrine (also known as adrenaline) and norepinephrine (also known as noradrenaline) are produced by the adrenal glands. These hormones help us think and move fast in an emergency and in the right situation, can save our lives. They don't linger in the body and dissipate as quickly as they were created. Cortisol, on the other hand, streams through our system all day long, and that's what makes it so dangerous.

The hormones that are released and the physiological changes that occur are designed to be a "spurt" and not present in the long-term. Stress prolongs these changes because the body believes that the threat is real. If we live a stressful life, we have then conditioned the body to believe it is in a permanent state of danger.

Stress Effects on Our Wellbeing

The physical and mental wellbeing is compromised by the permanent state of stress and the presence of cortisol in the system throughout the day. The result may produce psychological conditions such as emotional disorder, irritability leading to anger, a sense of rejection moving us into depression and physical conditions such as immune response disorder, chronic muscle tension, and increased blood pressure. These problems can eventually lead to serious, life-threatening illnesses such as heart attacks, kidney disease, and cancer.

Stress Effects on Our Mind

Neuroscientists have discovered how chronic stress and cortisol can damage the brain. Stress triggers long-term changes in brain structure and function. Young people who are exposed to chronic stress early in life are more prone, later in life, to suffer mental problems such as depression, anxiety, mood disorders as well as learning difficulties.

It has long been established that stress-related illnesses, such as post-traumatic stress disorder or PTSD, trigger changes in brain structure including differences in size and connectivity of the amygdala. Our brains are mouldable through the plasticity nature of the structure. Chronic stress can prevent the neuropathways, connectivity, and fluidity of the plasticity, making our brain structure rigid and less pliable.

The 'stress hormone' cortisol affects the neuropathways between the hippocampus and amygdala in a way that creates a vicious cycle within the brain leaving it predisposed to be in a constant state of freeze-fight-flight.

There has been much talk and indeed proof that through positive mental attitude supported by heartfelt emotions, people can spontaneously become well, healed and better. Old people can become fitter and fell younger, overweight people can become slim, depressed people can become happy, and the list goes on.

By spending a little time each day in a positive, heartfelt affirming meditation, we can change our subconscious programming from a negative to a positive outcome.

Meditation and mindfulness have been consistently documented as highly effective in retraining the subconscious mind, teaching participants to become more responsible in the management of their inner thoughts, beliefs for their health, vitality, and well-being. Two decades of published research indicates that most people who spend time in meditation or mindfulness practice report lasting improvement in physical and physiological well-being.

For more information on Meditation and Mindfulness, check out my website www.ThePositiveMind.ie

Integration of our Shadow side

We, as human beings, have a great capacity for darkness and evil. We open the door to allow evil to enter. Sometimes we do this unintentionally. Occasionally we are fully aware of what we are doing.

Nevertheless, we don't realise after we open the door that we may not be able to close it. In fact, most times we cannot.

Many of us believe that we are incapable of evil, and therein lies the destructive power of darkness. Every one of us has the capacity for darkness or evil, and there are no exceptions.

We can fool ourselves by denying the truth, but we are only fooling ourselves, and in that denial, we fail to grow and expand into our great potential.

Only when we are fully aware of our capacity for darkness and evil, can we also be aware of our great capacity for goodness and light, and indeed Love.

By accepting we have a shadow side as well as a light side, we gain an understanding in which we can recognise our darker challenges when they are presented to us. This enables us to manage our choices more effectively and more lovingly.

How to Use this Book

Since positive thoughts and positive mind provoking thoughts create a state of positive energy in the body, the benefits of having a positive thought-provoking idea at the start of your day is healthy and beneficial to your well-being.

Hold the book in your hands in the morning and close your eyes, pause for 10/20 seconds and breathe deeply. As you do this, allow yourself to feel the book in your hands, allow yourself to open the book on a page, by using your thumb or finger to identify the page.

You will notice a thick coloured inner cover in the book, this is where you begin.

The selected page will contain your positive mind provoking thought for the day, and you will be amazed at how it will resonate with you throughout your day.

Read the quote or inspiration with an open heart and allow it to permeate within you. Feel its essence, even if you don't accept the information, allow it to sit with you, within you, and as it does, it will begin to bubble up feelings and emotions that you were unaware of. Allow an opening in the subconscious mind for new information and feelings to run new programs that will change the course of your life to a more inspired and positive outlook on living.

If you use this book on a regular basis and the same page keeps presenting itself, ask the questions "What have I missed? What have I not learned?" There are no coincidences in the universe.

Mind Heart Connection

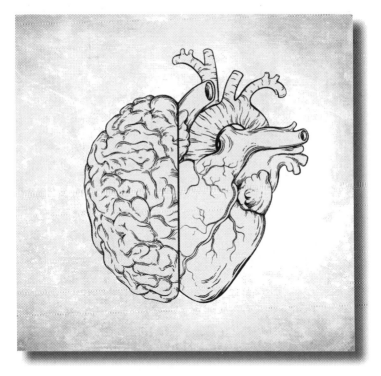

Mind Heart.

When we live our life from our heart space.

Our life becomes complete.

We attract into our lives what we spend our time thinking and dreaming about. Provided we truly believe that we deserve what it is desired, and we fully commit to the outcome.

Take care of your heart, become mindful of your feelings,
become intuitive - if it feels uncomfortable or wrong - It Is!

Trust the feeling.

Our subconscious mind is like a recording device, it records everything we see, hear, say, feel and do. It records our positive and negative thoughts, it records our great times and our traumas. It records all of these as images.

It then activates programs in response to those images without consideration of whether it's good or bad. These programs then get acted out by the conscious mind.

When we spend time in feeling, rather than thinking, we begin to recognise when and if the program is outdated or needs to be changed.

However, we cannot know this until we feel it and when we feel it, we can change it.

When we live with our heart open, we invite a connection between our heart and our subconscious mind.

This connection opens like a flower and absorbs like a sponge all that we can learn.

Gratitude

It's not just a word, it's not just a feeling, it's a heartfelt emotion of thankfulness, gratefulness, and appreciation. It is an acknowledgement that transcends words.

People who want to make changes in the world, usually do.

People who want to do good for others
and the world, usually do.

Are you one of those people?

Do you *feel* you want to make changes and do good?

Or

Do you *think* you will make changes and do good?

There are two immovable events in our lives that are, by far, the most important moments of our journey.

They are the moment we are born, and the moment we step into the next realm.

Therefore, everything in between is mouldable, moveable and changeable through our thoughts, feelings, and actions.

What sets human beings apart from other beings?

It's not our ability to use our intelligence, but our ability to communicate from our heart.

As humans, we value our friends and family. We want to build special relationships and have special connections in our lives, and that is great.

But a friendship that insists on their way in all things is not a friendship at all, it is a dictatorship.

Work from the heart and not from the mind, as the
ego pilots the mind and love pilots the heart.

An ego-driven mind can break a pure heart, but a pure
heart can also mould an ego-mind into loving perfection.

We as Humans are powerful beings, so trust in your own power provided it is fuelled from your heart and not your mind.

Power fuelled by the mind is a construct of the ego.
Power fuelled by the heart is pure unconditional Love.

How much energy would it take to use
your heart rather than your mind?

How much energy would it take to be kind and encouraging
to someone rather than being cruel and berating?

Find what you love to do in life, what career you love, where you'd love to live and who you'd love to be in company with. Have a passion for these aspects of your life.

Follow that path with all your heart. Do not allow the constructs of your mind to deter you from your heart's desire, for life without love and passion is not living.

The human heart and its pure essence of unconditional love is the guidance to our truth and future.

Sometimes people let us down, often they don't mean to.
But in truth, we often expect too much of others because we
expect them to do as we do, think as we think, feel as we feel.

However, they cannot - Because they are not us.

Be human today and have fun.

Do all the great things that humans do.

Be a being that is human.

Be kind to others.

Respect others no matter who they are, what they
do, what colour, creed or gender they are.

For they too are human beings, doing all
the great things that humans do.

Love life for it is your gift.

When we begin to realise that we create our present and future through our thought process, actions, and inner dialogue, then we realise that everything IS possible.

The light that shines in the heart can
illuminate any path of darkness.

However, we must connect with our heart to find that light.

Angels in the form of humans walk with us every day. We
don't know where they have come from, but we do know they
are here with us for a reason, we feel it deep within our core.

We accept that they come into our lives to carry
and support us when we cannot support ourselves
any longer. They come to guide us on our journey,
here on the planet, and then they leave again.

When they go, we can accept that it was their time to go and
we feel no bitterness or resentment, only gratitude for their help.

You cannot fail if you never try.

You can stay in your safe space if you never
try. Fear of failure can lock you there.

You can pretend that you are a success because you
have never failed, but in fact, have you ever tried?

If you have not failed – You have not learned.

The people who are quick to walk away are the people who never intended on staying anyway.

Real friends who truly connect with you and love you,
carry you and encourage you while never judging.

In return, your support and love can take
them into a different realm of life.

Life is a gift of living to be measured per second, not per day.

Don't put off something until tomorrow that you can do today, don't postpone that apology, for tomorrow may never come.

Live life to the fullest each day. Love with an open heart and enjoy the gift of life in every precious moment of every precious day.

What is your Heart's Desire?

Dream the dreams of your heart, follow that instinctive feeling that you get deep down between your heart and your gut. That feeling that you know to be your truth. You can only try, and maybe you may fail, but what if you fail to try? Is it not better to fail, knowing you have tried?

Whatever your heart desires, follow that desire. Your heart knows best. If you fail, at least you have failed trying.

When you do random acts of kindness or help another while respecting their dignity, you feel better within yourself.

There is no need to tell others of your deeds, just knowing of your own kindness raises your vibrational consciousness.

You begin to feel your heart lift with joy as you begin to realise your own pure potential.

From time to time we find ourselves drawn to individuals to carry them through their crisis. We often wonder why and yet we accept and continue.

However, so that we are not disappointed, we should not seek anything in return.

But we should accept that this was part of our agreement before we came on this journey.

How easy it is to encourage and support others,
rather than judging and berating them.

Encourage those around you to be the best that they can be and
in return, you will benefit from being the best that you can be.

Life is a journey of ups and downs. But when we live from our heart space and choose to care and love others, then others care and love us in return.

So our journey becomes beautiful, wholesome and we can manage life's ups and downs a little better.

Human beings are hardwired to touch and embrace
each other. Yet we live in a time where we are
afraid to show affection to each other.

We grow affectionally void and detached, yet a simple hug
can demonstrate empathy, caring, loving and connection.

Bear this in mind the next time you are
avoiding giving someone a hug.

Help someone feel connected again.

If we can honestly review our life from wherever we are now, this moment, and truthfully know that we had a positive impact on other people's lives, then we have lived a true and wholesome life.

When you feel that you cannot go on any longer
and the pain and sadness are too great.

If you are open to it, the angels come along and carry
you until you can make it on your own again.

Always believe in the impossible.

If we spend time gazing into the beauty of
nature, it invokes the miracle of life itself.

How every tree, plant, animal, and human are individual,
unique and yet connected as oneness through a matrix of
energy that spans the realms of time past, present and future.

Nothing can erase the pain of losing someone we love.

We carry that pain with us for the rest of
our lives, however long that may be.

The best we can hope for is that over time
the wound will begin to heal.

But no matter how strong we are or how hard
we fight, the scar always remains with us.

But also, their love remains in our heart forever.

Every conflict, no matter how dark it looks, no matter how hurt we feel, can have a resolution by taking time out and reflecting on all aspects with non-judgment.

Allow time for healing, become open and empathic of the other person's point of view, and allow forgiveness to resonate within the heart and then speak from the Heart.

First impressions are made within 0.35 of a second of meeting a person. We form subconscious decisions instantly, based upon our seven senses. We like or dislike in a heartbeat.

We don't get a second chance to impress the first time.

When a relationship is worth the effort, when it has a past worth saving, based on its pure core truth, no matter if it is business, friendship or lover, take the time to pause, feel, reflect and discuss.

Talking from the heart, without the ego, will heal the most broken of situations.

Life is akin to a kaleidoscope.

One change in direction, one change of thought, one change
in focus, changes everything in our present and future.

Not just the subject matter of the change, but all
the nuances surrounding the subject matter.

An interesting thing about our humanness is
how we cannot un-see what we have seen.

We cannot un-hear what we have heard, and
we cannot un-love who we have loved.

We can only choose to forget.

When life presents us with a second chance, pay attention, get some rest, reflect, be grateful and seize the moment with all that you have, as life seldom offers us a second chance.

Sometimes, the kindest, most loving thing to do (although painful) is to walk away.

Sometimes we are so great at helping others and
yet so poor at solving our own issues.

Yet, if we can realise that we create our own present and future,
then we know, if we allow our mind to connect with our heart
and feel the feeling in mindfulness, we can solve our own issues.

In my life, I have seen a lot of death, pain, and suffering. But I've also seen a lot of life, joy, and beauty.

I have experienced miracles that I cannot explain.

It is not the number of years that we live that matters, as our lives are an accumulation of precious moments, both positive and negative.

We never know where or when these precious moments will happen, but as they do, they etch into our hearts forever.

The smallest word with the biggest meaning

"NO"

When you say no, mean it. Feel it.

No is not maybe. Saying one thing and
meaning another causes confusion.

No is No.

Life, as we live, it is short, and yet we think it's long. It can change in a heartbeat. Sometimes for the better and sometimes for the worse.

Live each day as if there is no tomorrow, be present in the now, be respectful to all that is around you and be your true heart on this short journey.

A great wise teacher named Nelson Mandela once said:

'I never lose, I either win, or I learn.'

A valuable lesson imparted by an invaluable teacher.

When I reflect on my life, I see pain,
mistakes, failure, loss, and heartache.

But when I take some time to be mindful, to be present
with self, to sit in nature or sit in introspection, I
realise all I have learned, all that I AM and suddenly
I feel joy, truth, love, gratitude, and happiness.

INTIMACY -– In-to-me-see

It is not easy to allow others to see all of who we are when we struggle so much with accepting who and what we truly are.

But in the acceptance of self, we become intimate with self and therefore open our hearts for others to "Into me see."

Depression is our suppressed emotions.

Living out our lives not being true to who we really are.

But by being truthful to ourselves as to who we truly are, we can unlock our absolute true potential.

How many houses can I live in? How many cars can I drive? How many pairs of shoes can I wear at the one time? We live in a world of wanting more and more. The void in our hearts can never be filled with "the more" or "the want."

We can choose to ignore the signs, or we can choose to explore the void, painful as that may be.

If we choose to explore, we begin to journey inward on a journey of self-discovery. We look deep into our hearts to find what created the void and although this journey may be long and painful, during that journey, we begin to feel the connection of oneness. We begin to realise "the more" and "the want" is no longer the solution.

It always takes Sadness to know Happiness, Noise to appreciate Silence and Darkness to see the Light.

We live in a time where we seem to be more connected to each other than ever before with text, email, and social media.

Yet, we are lonelier now than ever before.

Every experience in life, every breath we take, everything we see, hear and feel are all awesome moments of the gift of our humanity.

When you find that special person, that person
you recognise in your universal knowing
completes you in a way you cannot explain.

Then you know how true love really feels.

A new day begins, what seemed dark yesterday is lighter today, and I am alive and breathing.

My angel rests beside me, and I am indeed, grateful for the miracle of life.

We experience miracles every day, even when we say we don't.

As we breathe in what we cannot see and yet trust that whatever it is that we cannot see, will be there for us every time we breathe so we can stay alive, is one of those miracles.

Some people form foundational elements in our lives. They form the bricks and mortar of who we are. They are so deeply embedded in our lives, and yet we take their existence for granted. Until they are suddenly no longer with us and pain grips us never like before.

In such times, we must find the strength to build on that solid foundation that was so generously provided for us. We become the bricks and mortar of strength, courage, and integrity for the next generation.

Being grateful for the gift that was given to us by those that formed those foundational elements.

When bad things happen, we blame everyone including God.

When good things happen, who do we thank?

What if I fail to succeed?

What if I succeed to fail?

I tried!

The ego mind brings us closer to arrogance while
the pure heart brings us closer to love

Mind = ego self

Heart = heart self

But also remember that the ego is imperative to our survival
on the planet, so be gentle with the ego and connect your
mind with your heart and be at one with all the facets of you.

Our heart feelings are never wrong!

Why?

Because our pure intelligence is in our heart
and our heart will never lead us astray

When the mind is congruent with the heart

the body becomes a temple of peace.

When I am grateful for all I have,

then,

I will have all I have ever needed.

When we smile, we release serotonin into our brain, and we begin to feel better about ourselves.

When we smile, others smile back, and they begin to feel better about themselves.

There is no cost in smiling, and yet by smiling, we can help ourselves and others alike.

I think it so, therefore, AM I?

I feel it in my heart,

Therefore, I AM.

Random acts of kindness increase our levels of serotonin and enhance our immune system, we feel better as a result, and the people that we are kind to will also feel better.

So be kind today with self and others.

No matter how long we will live, there will always be more to be seen than can ever be seen and there will always be more to do than can ever be done.

Yet, we are sometimes bored because we have not found gratitude for all that we already have.

On our journey through life, we should not take more than we need.

We always only need enough.

The more we ignore our inner suppressed feelings,
the more we compound our problems.

Our subconscious mind will contrive to resolve the
conflict between the conscious and subconscious,
continually raising issues for our attention.

If we choose to ignore, we can become ill, but we
can choose wellness, so pay attention to the signs and
connect with our inner self to find our resolution.

Boys don't cry.

This outdated paradigm of belief serves nobody.

Boys should be encouraged to cry to express
their feelings through their emotions, so they
can grow and become loving men.

It is good for men to cry too, as in crying we release
the emotions that have been locked in our hearts.

Be the love you are seeking.

Affirm each day with feeling.

I AM LOVE, and you will become a magnet for love.

Think and feel your life into existence

The answers you are seeking are not behind
you, they are not in your past.

Your past has created your present, and therefore, the
answers you seek are always here, now, within.

"I can't" simply means "I won't."

"You can" means "You will."

Just let go of the fear.

Grief is not just the intense sorrow experienced
for those who have passed from this life.

Grief is also an expression of loss for those we have
loved dearly, who no longer love us in return.

The cells of our bodies are intelligent beyond belief.

They react to every external stimulus.

They remember every event both positive and negative without regard for whether that event was positive or negative.

Humans are Hardwired to Touch and Hug.

In recent clinical trials, hungry monkeys chose to have a hug over satisfying their hunger. Monkeys and humans have similar hard wiring. The human touch cannot be quantified. In clinical studies, it has shown that in a restaurant setting, the waiter who touched the diner was 15% more likely to receive a tip, than the waiter who did not. [Fig. III].

Another study found that students are three times as likely to speak up in class after their teacher pats them in a friendly way. [Fig. IV].

Yet, we live in a world where schools discourage teachers hugging or touching their students for fear of abuse allegations. In workplaces, it's discouraged for fear of lawsuits. When I was a child and played on our road if I fell and hurt myself my neighbours would hug and kiss me better. Men and women alike. Now one would be terrified to hug a child for fear of being accused of something dark or sinister. What has happened to us?

Isolation brings us to loneliness and to the brink of taking our own lives. Teenage and adult depression is rising faster than we can manage. Humans are hardwired to hug and touch each other. A simple hug or touch can be enough to sustain us and keep us connected to the world.

Consider giving someone a hug today or simply touch someone on the hand, arm or shoulder when collecting your change at the checkout. Make someone feel connected.

Suppression of thoughts,

leads to depression of feelings,

leads to distress in the entire body,

which creates stress.

Stress creates illness.

Express your feelings.

Our True Essence.

When we are afraid, fear leads us to a path
into darkness and self-destruction.

In fear, we journey into anger. Anger brings us to
hate. Hate takes us into suffering and suffering leads
us away from our true essence of who we are,

Love.

Be the truth of who you are.

When we allow energies to grow in our heart, which is stemmed from external environments which drive the ego mind, an incongruence grows, a conflict within the heart grows.

The longer we fear our truth, the cycle continues and takes on its own life.

Living our lives from our truth, being truthful to who we are, brings us harmony and happiness.

Forgiveness is the key to acceptance, happiness, pure love and the path to our awakening. While there are many facets to forgiveness, the main facet is to forgive oneself.

As we journey through our lives, we sow seeds in our thoughts, words, actions, and feelings.

Some we will see bloom, while others we will never know about, and yet, without exception, they will all have a ripple effect on the universal consciousness.

Gift of being Human.

Our ability to connect with each other, our
ability to love each other and how we sacrifice for
each other, transcends our physical form.

Whether by divine creation or cosmic accident,
we are here on this planet together.

We are human with all the greatness of our humanity and
with all our flaws and weaknesses of that same humanity.

Just as one cannot have light without darkness,
we cannot have greatness without weakness.

Nevertheless, we exist, we are here, we live, and
we love – and that is truly a great gift.

We can achieve whatever we choose to achieve.
Our goals and desires are all but a mindful feeling
away. WE CAN, if we dream, feel and believe.

Allowing our dreams to be seeded from our heart and
believing that everything we desire can manifest if we
believe we truly deserve what it is that we desire.

Those who truly love you don't care about the mistakes you have made in your past, nor do they care about the dark images you hold of yourself.

Instead, they know the radiant beauty that you truly are, although you cannot see that beauty. They shine a light for you when you are dark, they hold your hand when you are lonely, and they help you to repair when you are broken.

Why?

Because they LOVE you.

You can manifest your life desires and dreams but
be clear and specific about what you really want. In
other words, give attention to your intention. Feel the
feelings associated with having your desires fulfilled
right now. Let go of all doubts, fears, worries and
negative thoughts associated with your intention.

Don't spend time figuring out how something will manifest,
but pay attention to the outcome. Pay attention to the dream
and how the realisation of that dream makes you feel.

By paying attention to fears, worries, doubts, and negative
thoughts, it will cause blocks in your manifestation.

These fears and doubts include phrases and thoughts such as:
"Let's hope this works" or "I'm not sure about this" (doubt) "I
want this, but I can't afford it…" (negative counter-intention).
"This is taking too long, when will I get it?" (worry).

The primary barrier to effective, consistent
manifestations that prevent manifestations is "a
sense of desperation" and "trying too hard."

Visualisation and affirmations are powerful tools in
our manifestations, but endless repeating without
pure heart feelings suggests that we don't believe
our affirmation or visualisation will manifest.

Do the visualisation and manifestation with
feeling and attention to the intention.

Write it down in a manifestation journal. Believe what you have written to be already manifesting. Trust in the outcome.

Don't try too hard, instead, trust and watch
as your dreams become a reality.

Why do we find it so hard to forgive others?
Because we cannot forgive ourselves!

We set standards for ourselves that are simply unachievable
because of our childhood disappointment and disapproval.

As we grow to adulthood, those standards become the
norm. We need to realise that the programming of our
childhood was flawed and the real standard in which we
should be setting for ourselves is love and only love.

We need to love self, and when we do, loving
others becomes an adventure and forgiveness
becomes the new reality and normality.

Forgiveness is the true path for all of us.

With forgiveness comes non-judgment and with
non-judgment comes true heart love.

When we stop judging we begin to live through our
heart space and start to live in harmony with every
living organism on our magnificent planet.

When we live in harmony, there is no judgment,
there is only "it is what it is" or simply "isness,"
and in "isness", forgiveness is automatic.

Love is the key.
Our emotional energy is contained within every cell of our
body. Through the electromagnetic field, this energy is
extended into everything we do. Just pause and consider, every
emotional feeling we have is transmitted into our daily activity.

For example, when we cook a meal, the
feelings we hold - whatever they
might be extended into what we are cooking. Imagine
being angry and bitter while cooking. Then wonder
why there is a bitter aftertaste in the food.

Another example, if we paint a picture. Look at the
difference in the painting when we are happy, sad or angry,
the emotion expresses itself onto the canvas or paper.
Consider when we are in our places of work. All those
feelings extend into what we are doing or creating.

If we work in a people business where we deal with
customers every day, think about how our inner emotions
extend outward to those people. How we interact with
them and affect them, both in good and bad ways.
Our emotions are not just internal. They start in
the heart and then radiate outward. They affect
everyone and everything we encounter.

Our emotional energy needs to be expressed and
released so we can be free of the internal combustion
and stress that is caused by non-expression.

If you are angry – be angry. But be angry with who or what has made you angry, don't vent that anger on some poor bystander. If you are happy – be happy. But be happy with who or what has made you happy.

Express your emotions - Don't bottle them up inside.

FORGIVENESS - Our Path to Enlightenment.

We all have made mistakes in our past. None of us are exempt
from that fact. We all have intentionally or unintentionally hurt
people we have loved through our actions, words or deeds.

We then spend a lifetime carrying out random acts
of kindness for the people we have hurt in the hope
of forgiveness. But if we don't forgive ourselves,
we continue to seek forgiveness externally.

When we forgive self we then can forgive others, we then allow
them to forgive us and then we can accept that forgiveness.

We awaken to enlightenment.

Love what you do and love your career
If you don't...
Change it.

The energy behind our emotion is so powerful. When
we love doing what we do, the productivity of what
we do is amplified, as is the energy behind it.

When we hate what we do. The same
applies to the opposite and more.

The result, poor productivity, bad attitude, low
energy, low self-esteem, no self or work satisfaction,
and stress, creating unhappiness in our lives.

The past is a construct of the mind, blinding us
and fooling us with illusions of grandeur.

The heart, on the other hand, wants to live in the
present. No grandeur. No illusion. Just truth.

Look into your heart for answers,
not into your mind.

Everyone has a Dark History from their Past.

We have all done things that were wrong or shameful, things we are not proud of, and, I mean everyone. But the past is behind us.

The present is now, a time for us to reflect, forgive ourselves and to send healing to those who we may have hurt along our journey.

Guilt and shame are fear based, and fear holds us in darkness. So, release the guilt, shame and move into the present, into the future in the light.

Others will judge our past because they cannot forgive themselves for their own dark atrocities of their past.

They form judgments to deflect their own inner fear and guilt.

When we imagine our life and future with the full heartfelt feelings, belief, and passion, as we did when we were small children, our imagination can become a reality.

Believe, feel and be passionate so the imagination can manifest.

Give gratitude as if it has already manifested.

Remain positive without a waiver and see your heartfelt imagination become a reality.

The Light Force of the Universe is like the Great Sun.

Sometimes, we say "the sun is not shining today," or
"the sun is gone in." The truth is, the sun is always
shining, but depending on the clouds or location
it will determine whether we can see its rays.

The light of the universe is the same. It is always there,
always loving, always guiding, always showing us
the way. But sometimes we unconsciously surround
ourselves with clouds to block its energy.

Sometimes we choose unconsciously to be in the wrong
location or wrong place, where dark energy prevails, and so, it
appears, that the light is not shining on, through or within us.

The great sun is always shining. The light and power
of the universe are always connected with us. When
we feel we are in the clouds, we must choose to
consciously reconnect at heart level to return to the
light. Move from the clouds and out of the darkness.

Our Choices.

Why do we settle for less when we always have a choice? Why then do we complain about the choices we have made but manage to blame others?

Make a choice. If you're not happy. Do something about it. Don't blame others for your inability to choose.

We may find ourselves drifting along in a relationship unsatisfied and unhappy, feeling trapped or sad.

But we remain in the relationship nonetheless, even though we have a choice to leave.

The choice may not appear to be a choice at all, it may appear painful, and of course, it may be. We remain and make every excuse under the sun as to why we must stay.

The truth is, we choose to stay and then complain endlessly about how the other person is making our life a misery.

We have a choice.

No matter whether it's work, a relationship, going to a restaurant or being berated by the bank manager.

If it's not working for you, either work to make it work or leave.

It is a choice, even when you feel it not.

When life gets on top of you, bringing you down into the darkest and deepest recesses of sadness and despair, as it has done with me on so many occasions.

Someone will then tell me how I have inspired them or helped them in their life. When that happens, I rise from my darkness, and I become even stronger than before.

Every time you inspire or help another, it creates a ripple in the universe that will always return to you.

When we become angry, we lose our ability to communicate.

We get stuck in our mind when we need to move into our heart.

Take a moment each day to be grateful for your past, no matter how good or bad you may perceive your past to have been.

Your past has been your learning for your present.
Your present is your exam time, and your future is
your degree which expires into your past as soon as
you have received it, and so the cycle continues.

We are always learning.

Take a little time today, just a few moments, to pay attention to the trees. How do they look? Bare branches or beautiful leaves? Look at how delicate they are, look at how strong they are.

Look up to the sky, see the blueness, or the greyness, see the clouds, watch them float, or travel at speed.

How amazing it all is, and we take it for granted every day. What magic this creation really is.

Knowledge and Wisdom.

Knowledge is information we hear, read and
learn, which is processed by the consciousness
and stored in the subconsciousness.

Wisdom is that knowledge processed by
the heart and known to be truth.

So, when we are guided by our heart, rather than
our head, the information becomes real.

When we learn, hear or read something, we
must be discerning in our learning.

If it feels from the heart to be true, then it
is true and becomes our wisdom.

From the moment you arrived on the planet, your guardian angel took your hand and helped you on your journey.

All these years later, no matter what age you have reached, that same guardian angel remains by your side and is with you every single day.

Always guiding, always loving, never judging.

If we never experience sadness, how
can we experience happiness?

If we never experience hatred how can we experience love? If
we never experience darkness how do we know what light is?

Each time we experience – We learn to
appreciate and understand the opposite.

Our journey here on earth is not about accession.
It is to live fully and wholly on earth.

To live, laugh, love and enjoy life with all its gifts.

To learn from the human experience and cherish every moment.

It's about merger, balance and harmony and not to be "away
with the fairies" or spiritually perfect. Nor it is to be so
greedy and engulfed in the acquisition of material things.

We must live on the bridge.

That bridge is the heart.

The sun may be blocked by cloud today.

The same applies to the light as it gets blocked by corruption.

But remember the light is always present.

Today is a Great Day.

It is the day after yesterday that was filled with life
and learning, and it's the day before tomorrow,
the tomorrow that may never come.

So we only have the present, so live life to its full today.

Be happy and open your heart to the world
and all its wonders and mysteries.

As we ponder over what others have said and done to hurt us, we must understand that it was their ego, and not their true heart.

For when we work from our heart, we simply cannot hurt others.

Understand, forgive and live.

When we exhale, we never doubt there will be air to inhale.

We simply breathe.

When we go asleep at night, we never think
that we may not wake up tomorrow.

We sleep and awake.

We take so much for granted without even a thought.

Maybe we could consider all these gifts we have
been given and for a moment, just be grateful.

We meet people along our journey, Some we
befriend, others we choose to ignore.

Those that we befriend will leave when they have had their
fill of energy. Others leave when the going gets rough.

But very few stay for the whole trip, never getting phased or
bothered by the turbulence in our friend's lives. Instead of
always being there to be supportive, helpful and always loving.

Be grateful for those true friends in your life,
as they are few and far in-between.

As I grow older, I reflect on my life and days past. Memories of people, friends, places, things, and experiences.

From those, I can choose to remember all the bad things I have done, of which are numerous, along with all the negative things that have happened to me, of which are many.

OR

I can choose to remember all the good I have done in life, which outweighs the bad. The positive things that have happened to me, which are too many to remember.

Then I realise that there really is no choice at al,l only gratitude, as without the bad and the good I cannot be the man I am today. For that gift, I am eternally grateful.

The great ocean with its mystery, vastness,
and power holds our planet in balance.

Water we cannot drink or live in, yet we cannot live without.
This is the awesomeness of creation.

Mother Earth creates such beauty in the shape of plants and wildflowers, and for some reason, we call them weeds.

When you really pay attention to the pure beauty of wildflowers and plants, then you see the real beauty of weeds.

I would be honoured to be a weed.

Things We Can do Every Day to Feel Better.

We can dress well, have a shower, shave, wear make-up if that's your thing. Make an effort to look your very best.

Compliment at least one person every day. Say something nice to someone, build another person's self-worth. It costs nothing.

Use your manners. If someone holds the door for you, say 'thank you.' Why do we now think we have an entitlement to be rude. Rudeness is hurtful to others.

Smile at everyone. When we smile, others smile back, and they begin to feel better about themselves.

Don't dwell on your mistakes, mistakes happen so we can learn. Think about what you have learned from the mistake.

If you have hurt someone by your life goals, carelessness or thoughtlessness, say you're sorry. If you cant say you're sorry, for whatever reason, write it down and burn it.

Be yourself. Just be who you are and don't compromise yourself for anyone.

Be your heart and not your head.

Be truthful. Or at least don't tell lies.

No matter how long we live, even though that may prove a very long time, we must remind ourselves to love every moment of every hour of every day as if it were our last.

Life is too beautiful and too short to miss a single moment.

Judgement

We meet people every day. We form opinions
in our minds, we form judgements.

If we were to use our heart, we would see into the
hearts of others. See their light. See their potential. See
their darkness, see their weakness and vulnerability
and their imperfection and see their truth.

Instead of instant judgement. Pause a while, feel what the
heart is telling you and listen to that inner knowing.

Then follow your true heart in action. The
Heart will never misguide you.

Sometimes, we love blindly and give selflessly.

But then a pain grows in our heart because that love
that we have shared so freely is taken for granted.

The giving and our generosity become an expectation
of the recipient. Then those that have fed off our
kindness will usually hide and disappear from our
lives because of their shame or embarrassment.

But all the time we still love them, unconditionally.

Love has no conditions, no limits, no boundaries.
Yes, we get hurt, but it does not stop us loving.

When people have been kind to you, loved you and shown
you mercy when no others would. Taken you in, cared for
you, fed you, paid your bills, loved you and minded you.

Have a little selfless thought and show a little
gratitude by not hiding in your embarrassment.

Don't disappear out of the lives of those who love you.

They did all they did because they loved
you not for any other reason.

Don't go and hide.

That pain can be emotional or physical. Some of us actively seek out pain whether it be physical or emotional. Sometimes we learn from that pain, but sometimes we don't.

Others choose to numb the pain, so they don't have to face up to reality or take responsibility.

But what if feeling nothing is the worst pain of all and what if the sharing of pain connects us to each other. Reminding us that none of us are alone and we are all connected. We are all one.

If the experience of pain brought about the realisation of oneness in our tribal village, all connected as one, then that pain has served us well.

The Circle of Life.

Most human beings have still not figured out the circle of life. We take, ruin and plunder this great planet for our greed and insatiable need for more.

We take way beyond our quota - never giving back.

We show no respect for the circle of life or its creation. The more we have, the more we want.

We need to learn when enough is enough and realise that for most of us, we already have more than enough.

The Sweet Success of Failure.

Over the course of my life, I have been successful sometimes.
I have also failed sometimes. When I failed, I became
stuck. But I was never one to remain stuck for long.

So I would try again, and again, sometimes I was
successful and sometimes I would fail. But I had tried.

The times I was successful the first time around, what
did I learn? I learned success, I learned victory, triumph,
accomplishment. But I had not learned failure, nor did
I know how ether success or failure was achieved.

As I continued to be successful, I began to
believe in my mind that I could not fail.

As time passed, failure began to present itself, over and
over. I did not know what recurring failure was, but
now I was living it. So, I began to learn failure. I lived in
failure, I feared failure, and so I created more failure.

But, if I had not failed, I could not have learned.

As I failed, I learned and so could reflect
on the mistakes I had made.

As I reflected, I became aware that I failed from thinking
(mind) and I was successful in feeling (heart).

Now I have learned, and I feel, and therefore I am successful.

The "Always On" Connection.

The great sun is akin to the connection to source. Sometimes
the sun is visible in the sky, and sometimes it's not. No
matter what the time of day or the weather. The great
sun is always there. Just like our connection to source.

Sometimes we feel disconnected through our thoughts
forged by our ego mind. Sometimes we don't feel
the connection because we have consumed drugs or
alcohol. Sometimes we choose not to feel the connection
for fear of the revelation of who we truly are.

No matter whether we choose through thought or action.
The connection is always there. The love of our creator is
forever in our hearts. Perhaps, we could remember this the
next time we journey into darkness or feel alone and isolated.

How can the teacher become a teacher if he/she does not experience, learn, further experience and continue to learn?

It's through the learning, experiences and re-learning that wisdom is instilled, and it's that wisdom that allows the teacher to be a teacher

Paying Attention

We are reminded, as we look around, at the beauty of life and the beauty of living things, we only notice if we pay attention.

As days stretch into weeks, weeks into months and months into years, time can lose its meaning. We begin to drift along like a log on the ocean wave. Life can be busy with fighting, worrying, obsessing, working and surviving, so we spend very little time paying attention.

Pay attention to the smell of our own body, the smell of the air, the sound of the birds. The sound of the wind or the ocean, the sight of the clouds and sky.

The feeling of being, when in a forest or on a mountainside. But paying attention is far more than that.

Paying attention to our partner, wife or husband, what they are wearing. Do you remember what your partner was wearing the last time you saw them?

Paying attention to what they are saying or not saying, how do they look, how do they smell? Paying attention to our children or our siblings. Watching how they look, behave, perform, watching out for the tell-tale signs of how they are coping with life.

Paying attention to our friends and colleagues. Paying attention to our elderly. Are they happy or are they sad and how can we help?

Begin to pay attention to everything and feel
how fulfilling that can be in our own lives

Our body feels pain to warn us of danger. The brain
registers something is wrong and signals the pain
receptors to activate so that we will pay attention.

Human Beings are Heart Wired to Connect.

We are drawn to one another by our human
chemistry. We build natural bridges that bond
us, brain to brain and heart to heart.

Those bonds once formed are not designed to be broken.

Our brains, our entire nervous systems, and our hearts
are designed for us to form deep, lasting bonds. When
those connections are broken, the pain we feel in our
heart, although not physical, is as real as it gets.

Whatever you do

Whoever you are

Be the best you can be at what you do

Stay true to who you are

In time you will achieve all you desire.

The Miracle of Humanness.

No one can explain how it happened, whether by
divine creation or cosmic accident, that we are
here. We exist, and it's a true miracle, a gift that
is rare and beautiful and is to be cherished.

This gift, this miracle of life has been revealed to me
throughout time and space repeatedly. As I watch the
clouds race across the sky, as I listen to music and become
touched to my core with its melody and vibration.

As I see the ocean and its vastness, the power of
the waves and as I observe a baby pushing from
the womb, in its perfection and imperfection, fully
formed with intelligence, from a fluid seed.

These are indeed miracles of life.

They are gifts given to us by our creator. Yes, we can
use science to make logical sense of all we are. We
can strive to prove all that's verifiable. We can put a
spin on all of creation to demonstrate our origin and
existence, to prove our human greatness. Or can we?

Life is a miracle, and we really cannot explain our
existence. Our humanness. Our love. The power of
our heart, in our human connection to each other.
Our ability to care for each other, to have concern for
all creatures of our habitat and our great planet.

Our ability to love one another, to feel the feelings
in our heart for another human being or animal
transcends our physical forms into a space and place
beyond the knowing or understanding of mankind.

This space or the place I call the 'Universal Matrix of Love.'

When we begin our journey into who we truly are,
it can be difficult, lonely, upsetting, overwhelming,
magic, exciting, dynamic and awesome.

We rise and fall like the ocean on this journey,
never knowing what's ahead, but one thing seems
to be certain, going back is never an option.

Trust all will be well, as it will be.

Sometimes people can be mean to you, they can say hurtful words, and do hurtful actions.

But we must remember, they are coming from a place where they fear what they don't understand.

They wish so much, to be open and honest but are fearful of what people might say or think, so they vent their negative comments at you.

Remember, this is their stuff and their fear.

It is not yours, so don't own it.

Do you know how unique you are?

How extremely special you are?

How beautiful you are?

What a miracle of life you are?

When the creator made you, there was no mistake,
no error, and no judgement. You were created with
absolute perfection in all your imperfection.

It is our shadow side, our ego, that distorts our vision and belief.

Be your Heart not your Mind

The average person will say 4300 words to an average of 5.4 people in a day and yet we fail to communicate our simple basic needs.

I need. I am. I love.

[Fig V]

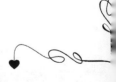

Trust the strange feeling you get in your stomach, called intuition and know you already know, what you need to know. You already know what's right and what's not.

Accept yourself as you are and everyone else will accept you too.

Be kind to yourself and love yourself.

You are so unique - as there is only one of you.

Have you ever considered the similarity of the cycle of a Crystal and the Human cycle?

An Amethyst, for example, is seeded in Mother Earth. It begins to grow - nurtured by the great mother and is influenced by its environment.

It grows to full beauty, radiant and vibrant, remembers everything and is unique in every way.

Eventually, it ends up back in the earth, sinks to the magma chamber, is seeded, and the cycle begins again.

As I watch the seasons change it reminds me of the
changes we all must make to live on our planet.

We cannot stay rigid and stuck in our
thoughts or stuck in our heads.

We must change and expand our consciousness.
Live our lives from our heart and love life.
Love each other and love the planet.

Energy cannot be destroyed, it can only be transformed.
Simply saying the words "Cleanse Cleanse, Cleanse" is just
not enough to clear lifetimes of our egos and abuse of power.

We MUST feel what we are saying, feel the
sensation in our heart, then we can release
lifetimes of karma and move into the light.

Light is constantly beamed into our souls, and all we must do is be quiet and allow the light to flow.

Flowing into our crown and finding residence in our heart.

Staying positive in the face of adversity expands our ability to absorb the light.

Today is the future of yesterday that we
looked forward to as tomorrow.

Today is the present.

Our present of bliss and life

Thank you!

When we carry the light in our heart, we illuminate
the path for others and realise there are so many parts
to the puzzle we have not been shown, just yet.

When we release our control over the outcome
and trust the process, we begin to know that all
is unfolding in perfect heavenly order.

Our choices in life have got us to where we are today. Without those choices, we could not be the persons we are today.

Our choices are powerful, even when it seems like we have no choice at all.

We always have a choice, we simply need to step out of our way to see those choices.

Our thoughts are powerful. Then we realise that
our thoughts are not inside our minds.

Instead they are in every cell of our body, but more
importantly, they are also outside our mind and body
in the matrix of consciousness - that space between
spaces, where all possibilities are present all the time.

Realise, just how prevailing and influential our thoughts truly
are, especially when they are propelled by heartfelt feelings.

As I walk my earthly journey and connect
with my divinity, I become lighter.

At the same time, darkness surrounds me, bringing
up to the surface new and old issues or habits.

As I stay true to my divinity, the light penetrates the darkness.
Light is victorious over the dark, and I am free once again.

Sometimes I become lost, I spiral downwards into the darkest abyss not knowing if I will ever resurface.

Time passes, I stay still, I learn to be accepting of this dark place and become at peace in the darkness.

As I am at peace in the darkness, I know I am held in the Light, and therefore I am not afraid.

I will resurface, and all is well.

Believe that the heartfelt imagination is manifest.

Give gratitude.

Remain positive without waiver and see
your imagination manifest.

We get stuck in the old programs, even when they are outdated. For us to move forward, we must change the programs in the subconscious mind.

We do this by reprogramming the mind with heartfelt affirmations and feelings.

Affirm the change that you want to experience.

I think, therefore, I am - René Descartes

Could we consider

I feel and think. Therefore, I am.

We now know that thoughts and feelings in alignment, heart and mind in alignment, is what makes "I feel and think. Therefore, I am" a more congruent statement.

How we think and how we feel creates our state of being, a state of I AM.

The mind sends out a signal into the quantum field.

The quantum field is the space between space where all possibilities and all potentialities exist.

The heart, on the other hand, sends out a magnetic signal into the quantum field that draws that energy and potentiality back onto itself.

Use your Heart – Not your mind.

Arrogance is fed from the egotistical mind.

Confidence is fuelled by deep heartfelt wisdom.

What did you notice last? When did
you previously pay attention?

We miss so much as we have become so busy, stressed and
connected to disconnection. Simple things pass us by,
such as, our partners grow older and we didn't notice.

Our partners want to leave us, and we wonder,
why? Our children grow up, and we wonder, what
happened? A small act of mindfulness each day
can keep you focused, keep you in the now.

Listen to the birds sing, yes, they still sing everywhere.
Look at the trees and really notice the tree, its
bark, branches, smell, colour, and texture.

Take a slow walk in nature and see what you can see.

Small acts of attention each day will allow
you to come back to the here and now.

Life is not about the destination

but the beautiful journey to take us there.

Did you ever notice how good you feel when you do a random act of kindness for another person? Did you ever notice how happy the other person looks as a result?

When you do random acts of kindness, serotonin is released in the brain, and you feel better, and so does the other person.

Set out to do a random act of kindness today
and feel the difference it makes.

If you never have experienced hardship,

how would you know comfort and ease?

Consider these aspects when you want to employ positive mind techniques to get what you want.

What exactly do I want?

Will I be happy when I get what I want?

Will I be content with what I want?

If I get what I want will it bring me closer to peace?

If I get what I want will it take me further from peace?

If I get what I want will it positively impact the lives of those around me?

If I get what I want will anyone get hurt?

Our Ancestor's

Most of our ancestors had a hard journey. They suffered hardship, strife, pain, grief, and misery.

We never give that a thought.

We could not be who we are or where we are today, without the sacrifices that our ancestors made.

Maybe we could be grateful to all those that have gone before us, for they have paved the way for the place we are in today.

There is a balance that must be adhered to for us
to have a harmonious and balanced life.

So, in the balance, err on being a giver and not a taker.

When we give from our heart, the recipient receives and in
turn their heart opens so that they too become giving.

Suggestions for Positive Healthy Living

Stand up tall and straight with your shoulders back –
You will feel taller, more present, and more alive.

Treat yourself like someone you are responsible for
helping – It's time for you to take responsibility for you.

Befriend people who want the best for you – Lose the people
that belittle you and cause you pain, hurt and sadness.

Compare yourself to you – Don't compare yourself to other
people, they are not you. If you must compare yourself
at all, compare yourself to who you were yesterday.

Suggestions for Positive Healthy Living

Analyse yourself before you criticise others – It's so easy
to criticise others for your own shortfalls and failings.

Tell the truth – Be as honest as you can, or at least don't lie.

Listen to others with interest - Assume the person
you are listening to knows something you don't.

Say what you mean and mean what you
say - Be precise in your speech.

People will promise never to leave you.

They will.

It's okay to be sad when they do.

It is always okay to cry.

Always!

Find a bathroom, bury your face in your pillow or cry in the shower.

Cry in the car. Cry when you need to or cry with friends and let it out.

Ignore what people say when they're angry.

When you make up, and they tell you that they didn't
mean any of it - always know that they did.

Also, know that they wish they didn't say it or mean it.

Forgive them.

Never pretend to be someone you're not.

If you don't like tea and classic novels, don't
act like you do to impress people.

If you don't want to wear leather jackets and combat
boots, don't wear them to please someone else.

If you are a boy and like boys, don't pretend to like girls,
don't pretend just because it might embarrass the family.

Be your truth.

Be true to yourself.

People will be mean to you, they will spread lies, call you names, and talk about you behind your back.

You will be hurt because you will not understand why.

If your vulnerability allows you to be open, you will realise that it was their issues, their stuff, their baggage and really nothing to do with you at all.

We hold up a mirror for others to see their own issues, and as we reflect those issues, we become vulnerable, and in that vulnerability, we learn.

Your friends will not always be there for you.

When you really need to talk, they may
not want to hear, and that's hard.

But that's okay.

Take a deep breath and remember all the
times you felt the same way.

Our life journey is interesting

We will wait, wait and wait for our first kiss,
our first date, and our first relationship.

The anticipation will kill us.

We will keep trying to find the right
person in everyone we meet.

But there's no rush.

The best things in life happen unplanned.

Enjoy being young.

Love that everything is spontaneous.

As we get older, things become more and more scheduled.

Embrace the fact that you aren't there yet.

Tell people how you really feel.

It will be terrifying in some cases and gratifying in others.

It will create relationships and ruin them.

But speak your heart, even if your voice shakes, because your heartfelt feelings may never otherwise be heard, tell the truth.

Sleep.

If you go to bed late, sleep in.

If you're still tired when you wake up, go back to bed. If you can't stay awake during the day, take a nap. Sleeping is a foolproof way of getting rid of your problems for a little while.

Utilize it.

Talk to people.

Talk to your sister about the guy she likes.

Talk to your brother about college.

Talk to your mom about her childhood.

Talk to your dad about his favourite books.

Talk to your grandparents about their families.

Talk to your friends, talk to your pets, talk to
the cute waitress/waiter at the restaurant.

Learn things from them. Always assume
others know something you don't.

Be inspired.

Take care of yourself. Wash your hair with that good smelling soap you love. Eat fruits and vegetables. Drink lots of water. Go for long walks in pretty parks.

There will always be someone prettier, smarter, funnier, or more popular than you. The beauty of it is that it isn't a competition.

Live with honour and integrity, even when others around you are liars and cheats, later in life you will realise the value of honesty.

Be yourself.

Make a choice,

If you're not happy,

Do something about it.

Don't blame others for your inability to choose.

Being authentic is a lifetime process of growth, healing, and loving ourselves as we become who we truly are.

As we truly express our authentic selves, through growth, healing, and self-love, we will also have moments that trigger our inner wounds.

We then may find ourselves acting in a way that is incongruent with our inner truth, and this is a reaction to our wounds being reopened.

When we become aware this is happening, we can reset and become our true authentic selves again.

We are all light and dark,

We all can be both good and bad.

Our darkness is part of us, part of who we truly
are, not to be feared, but to be embraced.

Dance with the shadow.

Sometimes we hurt the people we love.

We sometimes try to fix the hurt that we have
caused, by always being there for the person,
by always helping without being asked.

But all the time we are being resented for our efforts because
we have not allowed the other person to grow and heal.

You are unique in every way,

You are not the same as anyone else,

You may appear to be the same,

But you are not.

So, why would you want to emulate someone else?

Be yourself.

You can never lose who you are

Sometimes you go into hiding when you become
vulnerable and unable to navigate your way

The energy on the planet is thick and heavy

And sometimes we need to just rest

But we can never lose who we really are.

Believe what your heart knows to be the truth

Don't think, just feel

Move from your mind into your Heart

See how it feels

Know what's true

Sometimes we stand on the coat-tails of others

Sometimes we stand on the shoulders of our hero's

But you stand tall on your own two feet when
you have pure truth in your Heart

Love with tenderness

Be open and honest

Don't break other people's hearts out of carelessness

Don't allow others to be careless with your Heart

Our Hearts are precious.

Become friends with your Ego

But know how the Ego is formed, firstly

The Id is our Child-like self-centred, primitive aspect of self

The Ego is the decision maker

The Super Ego manages our moral and ethical responsibility

Sometimes we get stuck in the Id, we throw a
tantrum, throw the rattler out of the pram.

But now you are aware what aspect of
you is having the tantrum.

Appendix

Fig 1 2012: https://www.brucelipton.com/resource/interview/interview-bruce-planeta-magazine-part-3

Fig II 2004: PNAS 101(49): 17312-17315

Fig III 1998: Lynn, M. Reach out and touch your customers [Electronic version]. Cornell Hotel and Restaurant Administration Quarterly, 39(3), 60-65. Retrieved [27062018], from Cornell University, School of Hospitality Administration site:http://scholarship.sha.cornell.edu/articles/112

Fig IV 2004: Social Psychology of Education 7: 89–98.

Fig V 2007: Watts, Nick, The Human Footprint

Fig VI 1637: Descartes, Rene, The *Discourse on The Method*

Printed in the United States
By Bookmasters